PAUL HUMANN

GALAPAGOS
A Terrestrial and Marine Phenomenon

EDICIONES LIBRI MUNDI
ENRIQUE GROSSE-LUEMERN

To my Parents, "Turk" and Glendora

1988 Galapagos A Terrestrial and Marine Phenomenon
    Copyright © Paul Humann
    © Sipimex - Chile
    © Ediciones Libri - Mundi Enrique Grosse - Luemern, Quito, Ecuador

1994 Second Edition:
    Copyright © Paul Humann
    © Ediciones Libri - Mundi Enrique Grosse - Luemern, Quito, Ecuador

Editors: Patricia Reilly - Collins and Ned De Loach
Art & Design: Paul Humann and Sipimex, Chile

The publication of the map of Galapagos islands has been authorised for this book according to written communication 880057-IGM-G-6 (0267) dated 19th February 1988, at Quito-Ecuador.

Colour Separations by Machado Ltda., Chile
Typography by Sipimex Ltda., Chile
Printing by Imprenta Mariscal, Quito-Ecuador

ISBN 9978-9902-3-2
ISBN 1-878348-09-4

Ediciones Libri-Mundi Enrique Grosse-Luemern
Juan León Mera 851
Fax: 5932 504-209
P.O. BOX 17-01-3029
Quito-Ecuador

All rigths reserved.

No part of this book may be reproduced prior wittten consent.

ACKNOWLEDGEMENTS

I appreciate the support of the many friends who have helped with this book. I would especially like to thank all the naturalist guides who have assisted me over the years in Galapagos. They made each trip a new, educational adventure and, consequently are responsible for much of this book's contents. Special credit should be given to my former guide, Michael Jackson, whose own book, *GALAPAGOS - A Natural History Guide,* 1985, is a fountain of information that I highly recommend to every visitor. Another former guide, Chris McFarling, read the text for accuracy. Tui DeRoy and Mark Jones of Academy Bay have been close and helpful friends. Tui's own book, *GALAPAGOS - Islands Lost in Time,* 1980, is a phenomenal photographic essay of the Islands and the flora and fauna found above water. My friend, cinematographer Howard Hall, was with me during the sperm whale expedition and provided the wonderful underwater photograph of penguins, page 51. I have spent many happy days with fellow photographer and close friend Feodor Pitcairn in Galapagos. I must admit that it was, in part, his joking taunts that motivated this book. I would like to thank Carl Roessler, of See & Sea Travel in San Francisco, who made many of my trips to Galapagos possible.

Henk W. Kasteleijn, with the Charles Darwin Research Station and Gary Robinson, formerly with the Station, provided many of the scientific identifications of marine life. Dr. John McCosker of the California Academy of Sciences, Steinhart Aquarium, and Dr. Richard Rosenblatt of the Scripps Institution of Oceanography, helped with the scientific identifications of fish. Any mistakes in scientific or other information, however, are my sole responsibility.

Paul Humann

TABLE OF CONTENTS

THE GALAPAGOS ARCHIPELAGO: VI
  A World Resource by Frank Boren
  President, The Nature Conservancy

INTRODUCTION VII

LANDSCAPES IX
  Text X
  Color Plates 1–16
  Picture Captions XI

SEASCAPES XIII
  Text XIV
  Color Plates 17–32
  Picture Captions XV

REPTILES XVII
  Text XVIII
  Color Plates 33–48
  Picture Captions XIX

BIRDS XXI
  Text XXII
  Color Plates 49–64
  Picture Captions XXIII

PLANTS XXV
  Text XXVI
  Color Plates 65–80
  Picture Captions XXVII

MARINE MAMMALS AND OTHER SUBJECTS XXIX
  Text XXX
  Color Plates 81–96
  Picture Captions XXXI

FISH XXXIII
  Text XXXIV
  Color Plates 97–112
  Picture Captions XXXV

MARINE INVERTEBRATES XXXVII
  Text XXXVIII
  Color Plates 113–128
  Picture Captions XXXIX

THE GALAPAGOS ARCHIPELAGO: A WORLD RESOURCE

By Frank Boren
President of The Nature Conservancy

Paul Humann's GALAPAGOS is a remarkable voyage into one of the most unique natural systems in the world. For the seasoned Galapagos traveler or for the yet uninitiated, Mr. Humann's book brings home the riches that Darwin first brought to the world's attention, the wonder that is the Galapagos.

The Galapagos Archipelago is home to an array of plant and animal life found nowhere else in the world. The colonizing life forms each arrived with, and survived because of, adaptive traits which allowed them to endure the isolated, rugged land and seascapes.

The result: delicately integrated terrestrial and marine ecosystems. The remote Galapagos Islands are the world's living model of adaptation and survival which shaped a basic premise of modern human thought: the theory of evolution.

Over the past century and a half, many changes have occurred in the Galapagos, changes related to increasing human influence on the islands. From the degradation wrought by sailors and early colonists to the stresses of modern tourism, survival pressures on the indigenous wildlife are increasing. While expanding tourism is a boon to the conservation of the Galapagos through the attention and financial support it generates, it creates its own conservation challenges, especially in regularly visited areas.

An equally worrisome threat is the introduction of plants and animals from other areas of the world. Insulated from outside influences, the creatures that inhabit the islands are faced with unaccustomed competition pressures from introduced species. Over the years the species arriving with sailors and colonists have wreaked havoc on the indigenous populations. Having evolved in isolation, many of the native plants and animals cannot compete successfully with feral populations of dogs, goats, pigs, or rats. Some native species have succumbed to direct predation and competition for food. Today's greatest conservation challenge in the Galapagos is to prevent outside influences from causing the extinction of its unique native life forms.

In response to the rapidly declining ecological conditions in the Galapagos, a group of international scientists met in Belgium in 1959 to found the Charles Darwin Foundation. The Charles Darwin Foundation is an organization dedicated to the conservation and preservation of the natural environment of the islands and the surrounding seas. Also in 1959, the Galapagos Islands were formally declared a national park by the Government of Ecuador and the Galapagos National Park Service was formed. Over the next few years, the Charles Darwin Research Station (CDRS) was established to work in partnership with the Galapagos National Park Service to preserve the archipelago. Today ninety-eight percent of the total land area of the Galapagos is national park land. In 1986, recognizing the importance of the marine ecosystem to the integrity of the Galapagos, the Government of Ecuador declared the waters surrounding the islands a marine reserve, thus providing protection for thousands of unique and endemic species from whales to algae.

The mission of the CDRS is to promote a return to the natural ecological processes and to preserve the Galapagos for future generations. To accomplish this, the CDRS acts in a scientific advisory capacity. Visiting international scientists conduct advanced research at the Station. In a unique cooperative management effort, the Galapagos Park Service then taps the scientists' expertise and technical advice to plan and implement innovative solutions to the island's many distinct management problems.

Station activities include management of native species for breeding and reintroduction programs; elimination of introduced animals; scientific studies and surveys of plant and animal species; providing advice for developing the management plan for the marine reserve; and general monitoring of the overall ecology of the islands. Additionally, the Station is responsible for helping to train naturalist tour guides who accompany all visitors to the Galapagos and for the public environmental education program for schools and the general public.

Until recently, the Station relied on the generosity of individuals, foundations, and governments to provide its income; no core of funds to provide a permanent and reliable means of income existed. The monetary resources available to the Station varied greatly with changing economic climates. Unpredictable fluctuations in cash flow resulted in the interruption or curtailment of management programs vital to the conservation objectives of the CDRS and the Park Service. Critical to the successful conservation of the biological processes of this living laboratory is continuity in the study and management of the islands.

In an effort to provide the stability and continuity needed for the Station to succed in its mission, the Smithsonian Institution and The Nature Conservancy launched a $ 1.5 million endowment campaign for the Galapagos Islands in 1985. The interest earned by the endowment fund, while not enough to solve all of the financial needs of the Station, would guarantee a portion of the Station's budged annually. Thanks to the enthusiastic and generous giving of supporters from all over the world, The Nature Conservancy achieved its campaign goals in May of 1987. The endowment is now managed by the Darwin Scientific Foundation, Inc., incorporated specifically to manage the investments of the endowment fund, and the stabilizing factor essential to the Station's work of protecting the Galapagos environment and its inhabitants is in place.

The challenges facing successful restoration, management, and preservation of the Galapagos Islands and the marine reserve continue, however. To accomplish the full conservation agenda before us, additional support is mandatory. The fundraising effort to meet this challenge must be an ongoing concern.

With expanding financial support from the international community, with the financial stability of the Charles Darwin Research Station, and with the appreciation that a book such as Galapagos inspires, the understanding of this living laboratory will continue to increase and, thus, so will the protection of this incredible world heritage.

Frank D Boren

Contributions to the Galapagos Endowment Fund may be made to:

The Nature Conservancy
Galapagos Endowment Fund
1800 North Kent Street
Arlington, Virginia 22209, U.S.A.

or

The Darwin Scientific Foundation, Inc.
c/o The Smithsonian Institution
Washington, D.C. 20560

INTRODUCTION

The Galapagos Islands are located in the Pacific Ocean, on the equator, 600 miles west of the South American coast of Ecuador. There are 13 major islands, six smaller islands and numerous islets and rocks. Geologically speaking they are young, three to five million years, and are still considered one of the most active oceanic-volcanic regions on earth. The volcanic origin of the islands is obvious to any visitor from their appearance - basically an arid wasteland of craters, lava flows and ash. The archipelago is separated from other land masses by hundreds of miles of ocean. Additionally, the winds and ocean currents of the area generally act as effective buffers against outside intrusion. Only a limited number of plants and animals ever made their way to the islands and survived in the harsh environment. There were never any aboriginal people. Thus, the flora and fauna that did establish itself on the islands were left to develop without influence from the outside world, creating within the Galapagos Islands an isolated, natural laboratory.

The islands were discovered in 1535 by Fray Tomas de Berlanga, then the Bishop of Panama. For the next three centuries only occasional ships, primarily those of buccaneers and whalers, made landfall. They often took large numbers of the islands' huge tortoises and stored them to be used as fresh meat during their long Pacific voyages. There was no attempt to settle in Galapagos until the early 19th century. The archipelago's climate and terrain was simply not suitable for serious settlement and only a few villages were ever established. Even today there are inhabitants on only five islands, with a total population of less than 12,000.

Presently, although there is some farming and fishing, the primary source of income is from tourism. The majority of tourists arrive at the airstrip on Baltra Island. It was built by the United States during World War II. An additional airstrip was opened on San Cristobal in 1985. After their arrival, most tourists transfer to live-aboard boats - the most practical way to visit the surrounding sites of interest.

The islands are owned by Ecuador, which passed effective protective legislation establishing the Galapagos National Park Service in 1959. At present, 88 percent of the land is uninhabited and part of the National Park. Although man's intrusion into the islands may seem minimal, it has seriously affected the fragile balance of the ecosystems. Five species of rice rats and three subspecies of tortoises have become extinct. Many other animal populations have been greatly reduced. Land iguanas, once plentiful on Santiago and Baltra have been wiped out, although the species does still survive on other islands.

These losses were the result of both hunting and the introduction of burros, horses, cattle, pigs, goats, cats, dogs and rats. These feral animals destroy habitat, compete for food and, in some cases, directly attack the indigenous beings. The park service and the Charles Darwin Research Station are working to protect the islands from further disturbance by man and, insofar as possible, rid them of the feral animals and return them to their natural state.

The Galapagos Islands' primeval landscape of volcanoes and indigenous animals, who through eons of isolation never learned the fear of predation, are unique in the world. The tameness of the creatures is striking; nowhere else on earth can man approach and observe animals in the wild so closely. A significant amount of the flora and fauna is endemic - that is to say, not only native, but found no where else on earth. Consequently, for people who love wildlife, the islands are one of the world's foremost destinations.

The world-wide fame of the Galapagos Islands comes however, primarily as a result of a visit in 1835 by a young naturalist named Charles Darwin. Darwin was the naturalist aboard an English survey vessel, the H.M.S. Beagle, which was on an around-the-world mission and stopped in the archipelago for a five-week visit. At the time, with the exception of the many tortoises which had been removed, the islands were still in a relatively pristine state. Darwin was fascinated by the unique flora and fauna and studied it intently. His observations in Galapagos were the germinal stimulus for his theories of evolution and have forever linked the Islands to his name and those theories. Probably the most quoted passage from all of his writings, one that can hardly be improved upon today, summarizes his reaction to the Archipelago.

"The natural history of these islands is eminently curious, and well deserves attention. Most of the organic productions are aboriginal creations, found nowhere else; there is even a difference between the inhabitants of the different islands; yet all show a marked relationship with those of America, though separated from that continent by an open space of ocean, between 500 and 600 miles in width. The archipelago is a little world within itself.... Considering the small size of these islands, we feel the more astonished at the number of their aboriginal beings, and at their confined range. Seeing every height crowned with its crater, and the boundaries of the lava-streams still distinct, we are led to believe that within a period, geologically recent, the unbroken ocean was here spread out. Hence, both in space and time, we seem to brought somewhat near to that great fact - that mystery of mysteries - the first appearance of new beings on this earth." (Darwin, *The Voyage of the "Beagle,"* 1845).

LANDSCAPES

LANDSCAPES

With the excitement of expectation, I disembarked from my plane in Baltra; it was 1975 and my first trip to Galapagos. The sultry heat of the equatorial sun enveloped me - it was as intense as my disillusionment by the view. There was nothing in sight but brick red rocks and course soil. The monotony was broken only by short, leafless trees, thistle bushes, sunburnt brushwood and an occasional cactus. I thought, "this lifeless, barren desert is what I have traveled almost halfway around the world to see? Where is all the flora and fauna I had come to view in this, one of the world's most famous wildlife paradises - nature's own experimental station?" Then I remembered some of Charles Darwin's words: "The country was compared to what we might imagine the cultivated parts of the Infernal regions to be....Nothing could be less inviting than the first appearance." (Darwin, *Voyage of the "Beagle,"* 1845). Later that day, as we sailed from Baltra into the late afternoon sun, I read Herman Melville's description of Galapagos: "Take five-and-twenty heaps of cinders dumped here and there in an outside city lot; imagine some of them magnified into mountains, the vacant lot the sea; and you will have a fit idea of the general aspect of the Encantadas, or Enchanted Isles....It is to be doubted whether any spot of earth can, in desolateness, furnish a parallel to this group." (Melville, *The Encantadas*, 1841) Looking seaward, I could see the classic volcanic outline of Daphne Major. Close by was a sister islet, Daphne Minor - a cork shaped cinder pushing from the cobalt sea. Their stark beauty was floating in my mind as I fell asleep that evening and Melville's words kept coming back - enchanted....enchanted....

I awoke the next day to the sight of Pinnacle Rock, bathed in the golden glow of early morning light. It is an impressive monolith of volcanic tuff, its reddish hues reaching skyward 135 feet. This singular spectacle was but a foretoken of the bold landscapes to come. We took a short panga (the Ecuadorian name for small boat) ride to shore and climbed the 359-foot summit of Bartholome. There we beheld a spectacular view. Spread below was a scene of dramatic desolation formed by the residue of volcanic upheaval. Near and far were splatter cones, crags, crevices, pinnacles and peaks presenting an endless display of geologic patterns. Across a narrow channel of water was a huge flow of lava that looked fresh and new, although it was nearly 100 years old. In contrast to the spectrum of terra cotta browns, brick reds and amber golds were muted patches of green, giving testament to the fact that life indeed existed in this harsh environment.

The days blended as I continued to view scene after scene of harsh but unparalleled natural beauty. Each island has its own unique vantage point. From the top of the trail at Tagus Cove you can look seaward over a placid land-locked lake formed in a tuff crater and see your vessel floating in another tuff crater that has opened to the sea. Turn around, take a few steps and you overlook a massive lava flow as far as the eye can see. In the background, bathed in the purplish haze of distance and height rise the volcanoes named for Darwin and Wolf.

On Hood, you can stand atop a hundred-foot-high cliff and watch surging waves smash into the rocks below. Nearby a powerful blowhole powered by each succeeding wave spews water high into the air. A sea level chamber that connects by passageway to the surface sets the stage for this "aquadrama." As waves roll in, air trapped in the chamber is compressed and pushed out the passageway with great force, blowing air and water upward like a geyser. When large waves are rolling, the force is so powerful that the "whoosh" of air and water can be heard a full half mile away!

There are numerous untouched sand beaches found in an amazing array of colors and textures. Many are of coarse, black volcanic sand. In contrast, others are of fine, pure white sand, the granular remains of shells and coral. Volcanic ash has produced numerous sand beaches in hues of brownish red. A beach on Floreana even has a hint of green from olivine crystals eroded out of volcanic rock. Tortuga Bay at Villamil boasts a magnificent stretch of golden sand beach and constant rolling surf. It must surely be classed as one of the world's most beautiful beaches. The pristine beaches of Galapagos' are unpeopled, unlittered and unmarked except for the footprints of seabirds - they beckon exploration.

At several locations, well offshore from any major island, are great rock formations that spring upward hundreds of feet from the water's surface. The sky around each is filled with circling, screeching seabirds looking for prey attracted to this protective oasis in the open sea. Four-hundred-eighty-six-foot high Kicker Rock splits in two as it plummets to the depths of the sea. The opening is just wide enough for a sailboat to make a dramatic passage through the crack's length. Gardner, off the southeast coast of Floreana, has several magnificent natural arches that extend over the water before plunging into the sea. As you sail past, the islet of Watson comes into view. This barren outcropping of rock has three water-level tunnels that impressively pass completely through the islet!

Lexical descriptions of the Islands could continue into infinity. Suffice to say, the unique beauty of the Galapagean landscape simply captures one's soul - indeed the islands are enchanted.

4

5

7

8

15

16

12

17

LANDSCAPES

PICTURE CAPTIONS

1. A dramatic display of the sun's rays against clouds and sea.

2. A sweeping view of Santiago Island is offered from the heights of Bartholome Island.

3. From the heights of Bartholome, the view of splatter cones, lava fields and other volcanic debris is mute testimony to the geologically recent origin of the archipelago.

4. A sailboat traverses the narrow crack passage in Kicker Rock off San Cristobal Island.

5. Kicker Rock off San Cristobal Island is an impressive stone monolith, 486 feet in height.

6. Pinnacle Rock on Bartholome Island is a well known landmark that was once a part of a volcanic tuff cone.

7. Birds' footprints are often the only tracks one can find on the pristine sand beaches of the archipelago.

8. The runoff of receding waves creates a natural sand painting on the beach.

9. Espumilla Beach, at James Bay on Santiago Island, is typical of the unblemished beaches in Galapagos.

10. Puerto Villamil Beach, at Tortuga Bay on Isabela Island, rivals any bathing beach in the world, but is virtually unvisited by bathers.

11. The flamingo lagoon at Punta Cormorant on Floreana Island, during the overcast garua season.

12. Palo Santo trees, **Bursera graveolens**, form intriguing patterns against the background at Punta Cormorant, Floreana Island.

13. Cliffs and crashing waves present a breathtaking view at Punta Suarez, Espanola Island. Near these cliffs is the nesting site of a large waved albatross, **Diomedea irrorata**, colony. These magnificent birds use the cliffs as a takeoff point for flight.

14. With each succeeding wave, water dramatically spews high into the air from the great blow hole at Punta Suarez on Espanola Island. In the foreground is a male marine iguana, **Amblyrhynchus cristatus**, whose skin color becomes mottled red during mating season.

15. Devil's Crown rocks, just off Punta Cormorant, Floreana Island. The shallow water lagoon in the center of this circular rock formation is a favorite snorkeling spot among visitors.

16. Acting as gateway to the Galapagos, a natural arch dramatically rises from the sea just off the coast of Darwin, the northernmost island in the Archipelago.

17. A natural arch extends over the sea from Gardner Island and picturesquely frames Watson Island. Watson is a volcanic rock formation with three water-level tunnels that sensationally pass completely through the island.

18. Daphne Major during an El Nino, an unusual climatic condition which occasionally affects Galapagos and is characterized by warm air, seas and rain storms. As a result, the Island is unusually green with vegetation.

19. A view from the beach at Punta Espinosa on Fernandina Island. Isabela Island can be seen in the distance across Bolivar Channel.

20. Tagus Cove, on the west side of Isabela Island, is the remains of an ancient volcanic cone, now open to the sea. In the foreground is a stagnant salt lake crater.

21. A typically beautiful Galapagean sunset as seen from Seymour Island. Seaward is the cliff-sided island, Daphne Minor.

SEASCAPES

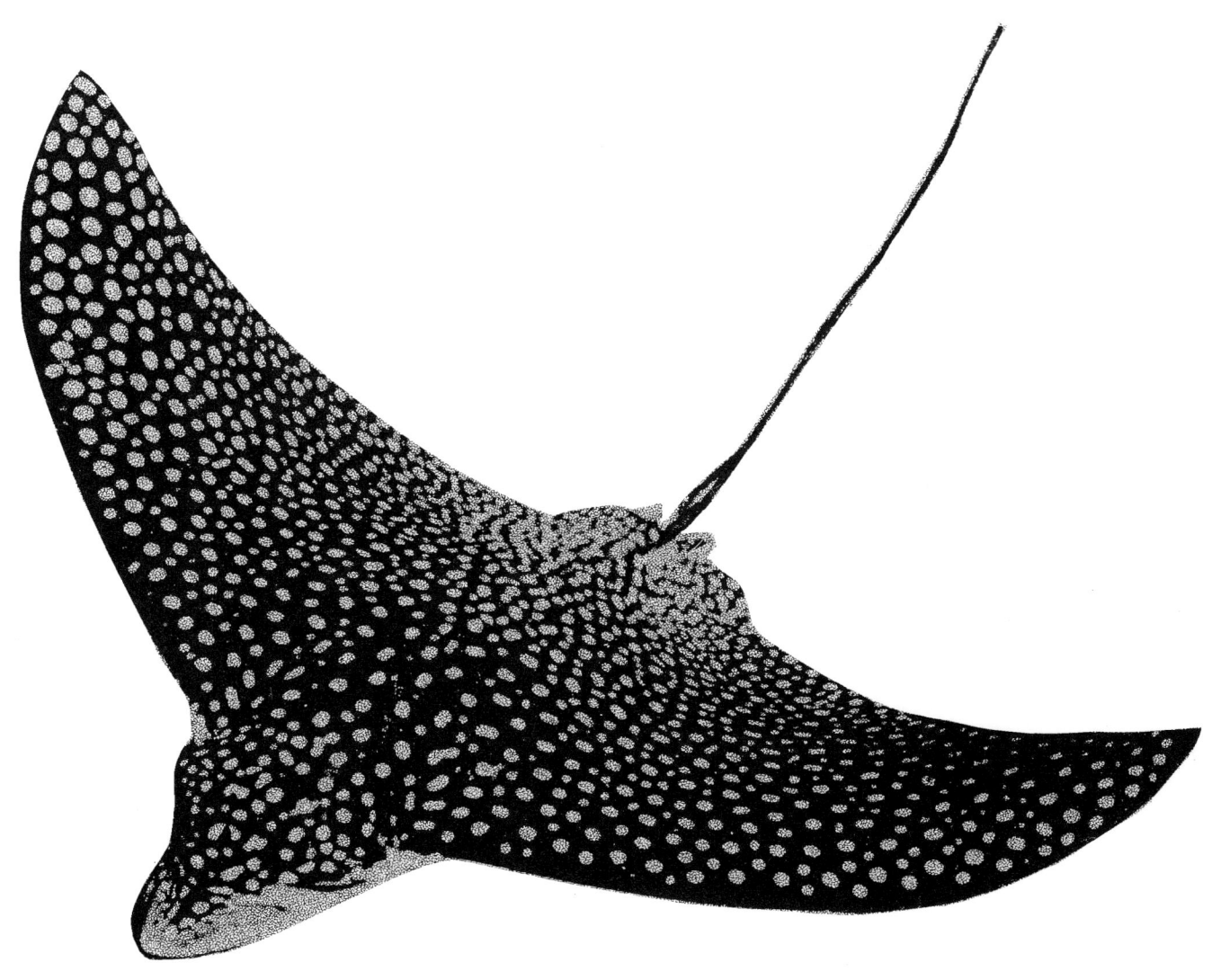

SEASCAPES

What Darwin and Melville may have suspected, but never experienced was the splendor found beneath the surface of the Galapagean sea. The underwater panoramas are as unique and fascinating as the above water scenes, yet belong to another world. Above water, the islands are basically a volcanic wasteland, with little flora and fauna. Only the fittest survived the struggle - so maintains Darwin.

In contrast, the underwater scene is rich in nutrients and teems with colorful life. Great schools of fish cruise the open water; at times they can be so thick that their shadow blocks out the sun. The reefs are an amazing profusion of invertebrate life as well. Swept by both cold-water currents from Antarctica and warm currents from the tropical Pacific, the marine life is a bizarre mixture of cold- and warm-water species.

William Beebe suspected the truth when he wrote: "Hosts of sally-lightfoots (tidal crabs) were the most brilliant spots of colour above the water in the islands, putting to shame the dull, drab hues of the terrestrial organisms and, hinting at the glories of colourful animal life beneath the surface of the sea." (Beebe, *Galapagos: Worlds End*, 1924).

I have experienced no other marine environment in the world where the unexpected happens on such a regular basis - exciting events are witnessed on nearly every dive. You can be swimming along a sheer underwater cliff with nothing special happening, when suddenly you are enveloped in a swirling school of silvery amberjacks, *Seriola rivoliana*, ranging from three to four feet in length. On other occasions you may subliminally feel the presence of something, look up and find a school of golden rays, *Rhinoptera steindachneri*, passing overhead, silhouetted against the sun's radiant glow. On almost every dive, one or more sea lions, *Zalophus californianus*, will burst into view like streaking jet fighters, then as if to show off, pause to perform all sorts of "aquabatic" maneuvers. Unexpected encounters might best express the Galapagean seascape.

By my ninth trip to Galapagos, I had acceptable photographs of most of the area's commonly observed fish. There was one glaring omission: the hammerhead shark, *Sphyrna* spp. I had seen hammerheads on every trip, but could never get close enough for a good shot. It seems that, generally, hammerheads are quite hesitant about approaching divers. I was determined to get a picture on this trip. As luck often goes, I didn't even see one the first twelve days of the trip.

On the first dive of the 13th day, I saw a school of hammerheads in the distant underwater haze. On the next two dives, I used every trick I knew to get close to the school, but my attempts were futile. On the last day of that trip, I spotted the sharks again and signaled my diving companions to take cover behind some large boulders. I hugged the flat lava bottom and slowly swam toward the school. Instead of moving away as they usually do, the school of 25 to 30 hammerheads suddenly turned and came straight for me! At first I was pleasantly surprised, but as they came closer and closer, I became a little concerned. This was a bit more excitement than I had anticipated.

Before I knew it they were all around me. My heart and adrenalin were pumping at full speed as was my camera shutter. My mind echoed one thought: "Keep shooting, this is what you wanted, idiot!" They made only one pass and were gone. Relaxing, I whimsically reflected, "Ah, yes, just another Galapagos diving adventure."

There are several strange looking fish in Galapagos, such as a sanguine frogfish, *Antennarius sanguineus*, and a goggle-eyed blenny, *Acanthemblemaria castroi*. Probably the most bizarre is the red-lipped batfish, *Ogcocephalus darwini*. As the name implies, it has large red lips that look as if someone got carried away with their lipstick. On the forehead is a unicorn-horn-like projection. Its pectoral fins have evolved into leg-like appendages on which it sits, with the tail making the third leg in a tripod-like stance.

Batfish are usually found sitting on what appear to be lifeless desert-like sand bottoms. At night, however, the sand comes alive. Consequently, one of my favorite ways to observe these strange fish is a night dive at Tagus Cove where the bottom is composed of coarse, dark, ash sand. At first it appears there is nothing to see; then your underwater light starts picking up life forms. Soon you find so many red-lipped batfish that you almost get bored looking at them. Next you start finding fish that are less apparent - those that blend into the background or hide in the sand. Snake eels, *Myrichthys Maculosus*, can actually move about under the sand, occasionally sticking their heads out to peer about. Pufferfish, *Sphoeroides* spp., bury themselves at night with only their opal-like eyes protruding above the sand. There are "winged" robin fish, *Prionotus albirostris* and small flat tonguefish, *Symphurus atramentatus*, that are almost indistinguishable from the sand until they move. Marine invertebrates are also in evidence. Tube-dwelling anemones, cerianthids, spread their delicate tentacles in a web of death for small creatures. Beautiful golden sand dollars, outlined in violet, forage about the sand for food. A night dive at Tagus Cove is always an exhilarating experience.

On one trip, I was cruising in open water back to our boat to pick up my cameras after finishing my group's check-out dive. Almost subliminally out of the hazy blue void, dark shapes began to form and appeared to be headed straight for me. The dim visibility prevented any immediate identification. They seemed larger than dolphins however - much larger. Then it hit me, whales!

As they drew closer, their size left no question and their bulb-shaped heads confirmed they were pilot whales. It was an awesome sight as seven swam in for a close look at me. Since I had no camera, I could do nothing but relax and enjoy the show. The whales seemed to move in slow motion and passed by so closely, I felt I could nearly touch them. They clicked and squeaked as their little black eyes looked me over. It was as if they were saying, "Hey, look at that strange one...will you?"

After just one pass-by they disappeared back into the blue void from which they had come. Although I was unable to take any photographs, there is an image etched in my memory, one of many such exciting images from the Galapagean seascape.

28

29

23

36

37

30

39

40

32

SEASCAPES

PICTURE CAPTIONS

22. A scuba diver is circled by a school of amberjacks, **Seriola colburni** (approx. 3ft.), a common occurrence off Champion Island near Punta Cormorant, Floreana Island.

23. A Galapagos shark, **Carcharhinus galapagensis** (approx. 7½ ft.), is seen cruising off Roca Redonda. When first recorded it was thought this shark was endemic to Galapagos, but it has since been found elsewhere. Above is a school of barracuda, **Sphyraena idiastes** (approx. 2½ft.), which are common in these waters.

24. A Galapagos sea lion, **Zalophus californianus wollebacki**, sits on a rocky ledge off Cousins Islet, near Santiago Island. In the foreground is a bush of yellow-black coral, **Antipathes galapagensis**.

25. Pacific green turtles, **Chelonia mydas agassisi**, are commonly sighted in the waters of the archipelago. This one was observed off Cousins Islet.

26. Golden rays, **Rhinoptera steindachneri** (approx. 3ft.), in formation against the sun off Cousins Islet are a breathtaking sight. These rays are rarely seen in offshore reef areas, but are frequently observed by visitors as they glide in large schools near the surface of mangrove lagoons.

27. Black jacks, **Caranx lugubris** (approx. 3ft.), cruise off Punta Pitt, San Cristobal Island. Below are golden-eyed grunts, **Haemulon scudderi**, and above are creole fish, **Paranthias colonus**.

28. An amberjack, **Seriola rivoliana** (approx. 3ft.), swims over gulf stars, **Oreaster occidentalis**, and pebble coral, **Cycloseris mexicana**, off Devil's Crown. Interestingly, pebble coral does not grow in colonies or attach to the substrata as do most corals. Instead individual polyps build disk-shaped pebbles of calcium carbonate that lay loose on the bottom.

29. Creole fish, **Paranthias colonus** (approx. 10in.), are among the most common inshore fish seen in Galapagos. Here they stream along an underwater cliff off Champion Island.

30. Schooling golden-eyed grunts, **Haemulon scudderi** (approx. 1ft.), are a common sight off Devil's Crown.

31. Schooling scalloped hammerhead sharks, **Sphyrna lewini** (approx. 10ft.), off Cousins Islet, are a rarely observed phenomenon.

32. Yellow-tailed surgeonfish, **Prionurus laticlavius** (approx. 1ft.), are common in the shallow waters of Galapagos. As seen here off Gardner Island near Espanola, their schools can be packed so tightly that they completely fill one's frame of view.

33. Schooling creole fish, **Paranthias colonus** (approx. 10in.), and bushes of endemic yellow-black coral, **Antipathes galapagensis**, off Champion Island.

34. Barracuda, **Sphyraena idiastes** (approx. 2½ft.), are usually observed in large schools as seen here off Roca Redonda.

35. Blackstriped salema, **Xenocys jessiae** (approx. 6in.), an endemic species, can pack so tightly that nothing can be seen through the school. They are common in the channel between Seymour and Baltra Islands.

36. Blending almost perfectly with the sand bottom is a tonguefish, **Symphurus atramentatus** (approx. 2½in.). This and all the photographs which follow in this chapter were taken during night dives on the sandy bottom of Tagus Cove, on the west side of Isabela Island.

37. The strange looking sea robin, **Prionotus albirostris** (approx. 3in.), and a conger eel (species not identified) poking its head from the sand. These curious eels can actually move about under the sand without disturbing the surface.

38. One of the most unusual appearing fish in these waters is the red-lipped batfish, **Ogcocephalus darwini** (approx. 8in.). It was originally thought to be an endemic species, but has since been found along the South American coasts of Ecuador and Peru.

39. Mating crabs.

40. A tube-dwelling, cerianthid anemone spreads its deadly, stinging tentacles to catch passing prey.

REPTILES

REPTILES

Ever since their discovery, the Galapagos Islands have been known for their giant tortoises, *Geochelone elephantopus*. In fact, the name Galapagos itself originates from the Spanish word "galapago," meaning tortoise. These enormous reptiles continue to be the best known of the Galapagos animals, and are often used as the visual symbol of the archipelago. Regrettably, they were brought to the brink of extinction by man, who hunted them for food, and by feral animals introduced by man into their habitat. Today they number only 15,000 compared to an estimated original population of 250,000.

Fortunately, today's visitors to the islands can be assured of viewing tortoises at the Charles Darwin Research Station. They are kept there for research, captive-breeding programs and viewing by the general public. The more energetic visitor can take advantage of the exciting opportunity of seeing these animals in the wild by hiking into the tortoise reserve on Santa Cruz, or taking an expedition to the rim of Alcedo Volcano, where they are still abundant in their natural habitat. Occasionally, a few lucky visitors experience the thrill of encountering these lumbering giants on established park trails.

It is the reptiles, in general, however, not just the tortoises alone, that set these islands apart from the rest of the world. Darwin poignantly wrote in his report on The Voyage of the "Beagle:" "We will now turn to the order of reptiles, which gives the most striking character to the zoology of these islands. The species are not numerous, but the numbers of individuals of each species are extraordinarily great…. When we remember the well-beaten paths made by the thousands of huge tortoises - the many turtles - the great warrens of the terrestrial *Amblyrhynchus* (genus of iguanas found only in Galapagos) - and the groups of the marine species basking on the coast-rocks of every island - we must admit that there is no other quarter of the world where this Order replaces the herbivorous mammalia in so extraordinary a manner. The geologist on hearing this will probably refer back in his mind to the Secondary epochs, when lizards, some herbivorous, some carnivorous, and of the dimensions comparable only with our existing whales, swarmed on the land and in the sea." (1845).

Twenty of the 22 species, or an amazing 90 percent of the reptiles found in Galapagos, are endemic (native and found nowhere else on earth). Only the green sea turtle, *Chelonia mydas*, and one of the geckoes, *Phyllodactylus leei*, are found elsewhere. Like other animals on the islands, the reptiles have no apparent fear of man and can be closely approached and observed by the visitor. The green sea turtle is relatively abundant in the waters of Galapagos, and of special international importance as it is considered an endangered species. Hunting of this species is prohibited and, in many areas, only natural predators attack the nests or young hatchlings. On some beaches, however, feral pigs and rats are a problem. Viewing one of these large reptiles underwater is a special treat. Generally, upon observing a diver, they will make a cautious retreat. If the diver makes no threatening motions, however, the turtle will often return and circle, obviously curious about this strange, unnatural intruder into the seascape. Occasionally they seem totally oblivious to a diver's presence.

Recently I took a new diver down to a rocky underwater ledge. The flow of currents around the ridge formed a natural feed funnel which often brought in large fish. We found an excellent vantage point at 50 feet. We waited on the ledge to see what exciting marine life might pass. Within a few seconds two majestic eagle rays came into view. I turned to be sure my companion saw the rays and was surprised to see a sea turtle sleeping right next to her. After the rays passed I signaled to my companion to look where the turtle lay. She glanced down and yelped with surprise. Naturally the commotion woke the turtle, who turned, looked at us, opened its mouth in an apparent yawn and went back to sleep!

The endemic marine iguanas, *Amblyrhynchus cristatus*, of Galapagos are the only iguanas in the world that feed underwater. Most of the time these tranquil but fearsome appearing creatures lie sunning themselves on lava rocks beside the sea. Once a day (usually between 10 AM and 2 PM depending on low tide), they will venture beneath the cold waters to forage about for marine algae.

One of the most difficult and challenging assignments for a marine life photographer is to get a picture of this unconventional feeding behavior. The shallow water is usually green and murky. To complicate matters further, there is almost always a strong surge in the area. More than once, I have been caught by the surge and tossed head over heels along the bottom, while the iguanas, with their long strong toes and nails, clung to the rock bottom and continued to munch away as if nothing had happened. In an attempt to stabilize myself, I strapped on 20 extra pounds of lead weight, and then crawled along the bottom in search of feeding iguanas.

Usually the iguanas will swim away when they see a diver, but with slow, unthreatening movements and luck, you can occasionally get close enough to take a photograph. Getting such a close view is worth all the effort, for they appear to be grazing monsters from prehistoric times.

43

44

51

53

56

57

58

59

REPTILES
PICTURE CAPTIONS

41. An endemic giant domed tortoise, **Geochelone elephantopus**, passes through bracken ferns, **Pteridium aquilinum**, on the tortoise reserve on Santa Cruz Island. Originally there were probably 13 races or subspecies of these animals, but today only nine viable races remain. Their total population is some 15,000, down from an estimated original population of 250,000. Hunting by mariners, and the introduction of feral animals, have been the primary reasons for these losses.

42. A huge tortoise, **Geochelone elephantopus**, seen here in the wild on Isabela Island.

43. Tortoise, **Geochelone elephantopus**, at the Charles Darwin Research Station on Santa Cruz Island, where a visitor can be assured of getting a close view of the huge reptiles for which the islands are famous.

44. The large tortoises of Galapagos are vegetarians and eat a wide variety of plants.

45. Mating "saddle-back" tortoises, **Geochelone elephantopus**, at the Charles Darwin Research Station on Santa Cruz Island. The saddle-back races were from Espanola, Pinzon, Pinta and Fernandina Islands.

46. Pacific green turtle, **Chelonia mydas agassisi**, on ledge with bushes of yellow-black coral, **Antipathes galapagensis**, off Cousins Islet. Galapagos is the only place in the world where the population of this endangered species is on the rise. This can be directly attributed to strict laws against hunting or disturbing nesting areas.

47. Swimming Pacific green turtles, **Chelonia mydas agassisi**.

48. The endemic land iguanas, **Conolophus subcristatus** (approx. 2½ft.), are native to the central and western islands of the archipelago. However, their populations have been wiped out on Santiago Island and Baltra as a result of man's activities. Most visitors view these prehistoric appearing reptiles on South Plaza Island, which supports an unusually dense population of over 300 adults.

49. Like their close relatives, the marine iguanas, land iguanas are tireless sunbathers.

50. Land iguana suns himself on the lava at Punta Espinosa, on Fernandina Island.

51. Land iguanas are vegetarians. One is seen here feeding on endemic **Sesuvium, Sesuvium edmonstonei**, on South Plaza Island.

52. Female lava lizard, **Tropidurus delanonis** (approx. 6in.), on Espanola Island, displays red markings on her head and throat. These markings distinguish her from the males.

53. Male lava lizard, **Tropidurus albemarlensis** (approx. 8in.), at James Bay on Santiago Island, feeds on an endemic scorpion, **Hadruroides lunatus**.

54. Endemic marine iguanas, **Amblyrhynchus cristatus** (approx. 2ft.), sunning themselves at Punta Espinosa on Fernandina Island. Sunning is necessary for them to bring their body temperatures up so they can digest food efficiently.

55. During breeding season, the male marine iguanas on Espanola display mottled red skin coloration.

56. Marine iguanas sunning themselves at **Punta Espinosa** on Fernandina Island. A small lava lizard, **Tropidurus albemarlensis**, is resting on the back of one of the iguanas.

57. Same as 55.

58. The marine iguanas of Galapagos are the only iguanas in the world to feed underwater on marine algae.

59. Marine iguana swimming on the water's surface.

60. Marine iguanas, with their long and strong toes and nails, cling to the rocky substrate while grazing on marine algae.

BIRDS

BIRDS

Because great expanses of ocean pose no hindrance to the migration of seabirds, it is not surprising to find a large population in Galapagos. What is surprising, considering their mobility, is that of 19 resident species, five are endemic. Take for example the flightless cormorant, *Nannopterum harrisi*, the only one of 29 world-wide species to have lost the ability of flight. They probably arrived on the wing eons ago. Then, with no natural terrestrial predators and feeding grounds literally at their seaside doorstep, the need for flight became somewhat unessential. Streamlined bodies for swimming proved more advantageous to their survival than the benefits of flight.

Another endemic anomaly are the Galapagos penguins, *Spheniscus mendiculus*. Penguins are a family of flightless seabirds associated with cold Antarctic waters. Thus, the Galapagos species seems completely out of place - in fact, it is the only species to nest entirely within the tropics and to be found north of the Equator. These cute little fellows, in their headwaiter dress, are the third smallest species in the world. Their closest relatives are the Humboldt and Magellan penguins which live thousands of miles to the south near the tip of South America.

With patience and luck, one can snorkel with the penguins while they are feeding near the shore on small fish. It is quite a sight to see their short, stout bodies zip about underwater, like guided torpedoes. It seems impossible that their small, blade-shaped wing remnant can propel them through the water so rapidly.

The magnificent waved albatross, *Diomedea irrorata*, is endemic to not only Galapagos, but nests only on Espanola (Hood) Island. It is the only one of 13 albatross species found exclusively in the tropics. Waved albatross are known for their entertaining and intricate courtship dance ritual, one of the most complex courtship systems seen in the bird kingdom. Interestingly, these great seabirds pair for life. They are heavy birds that have a difficult time taking off from land or water without sufficient wind. Consequently, their nesting sites are conveniently located near high cliffs over the sea, from which they literally jump off, attaining flight speed before reaching the rocks far below. There can be no more thrilling sight than watching one of these terrestrially clumsy birds waddle over to the cliff's edge, jump off, majestically spread its great wing span of over two meters, and soar like a sweeping sail plane.

The two of the three remaining endemic seabirds found in Galapagos are gulls. The swallow-tailed gull, *Creagrus furcatus*, has attractive, textured plumage, ranging from its black head through shades of gray to a white underside. The plumage is set off by red feet and a stunning, day-glow orange, eye-ring. It is one of the few gulls to feed out at sea in the night. The endemic lava gull, *Larus fuliginosus*, of which only about 400 mating pairs exist, is thought to be the rarest gull in the world. Their dark grey plumage camouflages them well on the lava rocks, where they are generally found. The remaining endemic seabird is the Galapagos storm petrel, *Oceanodroma tethys*.

Aside from the anomalies of the endemic seabirds, what probably impresses the average visitor most are the tameness and the sheer numbers of other seabirds. Boobies are the most common, of which three species are native to Galapagos. In all of the Archipelago, there is probably a no more surprising color than the intense bright blue feet of the blue-footed booby, *Sula nebouxii*. To the delight of tourists, these birds often perform their courtship dances within site of a trail. In fact, these birds are so oblivious to the presence of man that they will occasionally nest right on the trail!

The courtship ritual usually begins with the male throwing his head back and pointing his beak upward to attract the female - a display called "skypointing." They then do a slow, high-stepping dance maneuver where their foot action looks as if they were pulling their feet up off a sticky surface. Skypointing is then repeated by both male and female. With their wings cocked behind their heads, the male whistles and the female honks. Sticks and twigs are passed and placed in a ceremony that simulates nest building. Since blue-footed boobies do not actually build nests, this ritual must be a legacy of evolutionary history. All aspects of the courtship display may be repeated many times, the culmination of which is mating.

Another ground nester is the masked booby, *Sula dactylatra*, largest of the three. It has black wing markings and face mask set against brilliant, pure white body plumage. Its eyes are an intense yellow-gold. The red-footed booby, *Sula sula*, has a blue bill and as the name implies, bright red feet. It is the smallest of the boobies and, unlike the other two, nests in trees.

Frigatebirds are another tourist pleaser. There are two species in Galapagos - the great, *Fregata minor*, and magnificent, *F. magnificens*. They nest in low trees and shrubs, often next to tourist trails. During mating season the males sit in the nesting area and inflate their large, bright red throat sacs. As females fly over, the males throw their head and wings back and shake them vigorously while boastfully displaying their female attracting throat sacs. A loud, eerie warbling whistle accompanies this exotic display. Although they are primarily surface-water feeders, frigatebirds are true pirates in the sky. They are often seen in mid-air combat, attempting to rob other seabirds of their food. This activity gives them an alternate common name, "men-of-war" birds.

There are also many species of coastal birds, including the large, magnificently plumaged great blue heron, *Ardea herodias*; colorful, pastel pink, greater flamingos, *Phoenicopterus ruber*; distinctively marked, yellow-crowned night herons, *Nycttanassa violacea*, with large yellow-orange eyes; and, with brilliant orange-yellow-green eyes, the red billed American oystercatcher, *Haematopus ostralegus*. Of the coastal birds, however, only one is endemic - the small, dull gray lava heron, *Butorides sundevalli*.

Of 29 resident species of land birds, an amazing 22 species (75 percent) are endemic. To the average visitor, most are drab and uninteresting. To Darwin, however, they were much more. He was first surprised by their unusual tameness, noting that a gun was almost superfluous as the birds would often come close enough to be killed by a switch or even caught by hand alive! Of greater significance to his evolutionary theories were what have become known as "Darwin's Finches." Although they look almost identical, Darwin found that there were several distinct species - each with its own peculiar diet, method of obtaining food and beak shape. They are so much alike, however, that Darwin concluded they must have come from a common ancestor and thus exemplified his theory of evolution.

61

62

63

64

65

69

70

71

72

73

74

75

76

80

81

82

83

60

84

85

86

62

87

88

89

90

BIRDS

PICTURE CAPTIONS

61. Boobies catch fish by plunge diving, in a spectacular display of agility. These are blue-footed boobies, **Sula nebouxii,** feeding off Puerto Villamil, Isabela Island.

62. Endemic waved albatross, **Diomedea irrorata,** are often observed by visitors at their nesting site at Punta Suarez, Espanola Island.

63. Mating waved albatrosses.

64. Endemic Galapagos penguins, **Spheniscus mendiculus,** seen here feeding underwater off Sombrero Chino, Santiago Island.

65. Galapagos penguins, **Spheniscus mendiculus,** are the world's second smallest. They are the only species found north of the Equator and, which mate entirely within the tropics. These were photographed at Cape Douglas, Fernandina Island.

66. The endemic swallow-tailed gulls, **Creagrus furcatus,** are among the few species of gulls which feed out at sea during the night. This pair, seen on South Plaza Island, is preparing to mate.

67. This swallow-tailed gull, with chick, was photographed on Tower Island.

68. Masked boobies, **Sula dactylatra,** at sunset, on Punta Suarez, Espinosa Island. This species of booby is a ground nester.

69. A tree nesting red-footed booby, **Sula sula,** with chick, on Tower Island.

70. Red-footed boobies feed far out to sea and are rarely seen by visitors, except on Tower Island where they nest along park trails.

71. Blue-footed boobies, **Sula nebouxii,** perform a dramatic courtship display that starts with alternate foot raising.

72. During the courtship dance, the blue-footed boobies often have an endearing bill-touching ceremony.

73. The courtship dance continues when one or the other bird (usually the male) points its bill upward in a ritual called "skypointing."

74. Passing twigs in a ritual nest-building ceremony is thought to be an evolutionary relic, as blue-footed boobies simply clear an area on the ground to lay eggs; they no longer build nests.

75. A short-eared owl, **Asio flammeus,** seen here on Tower Island. It often feeds on nestlings of the endemic Galapagos storm petrels, **Oceanodroma tethys,** and Madeiran storm petrels, **O. castro.**

76. Endemic Galapagos hawks, **Buteo galapagoensis,** have no natural enemies and are virtually fearless, often coming close to investigate visitors. Charles Darwin noted: "A gun is here almost superfluous; for with the muzzle I pushed a hawk out of the branch of a tree." (**Voyage of the "Beagle,"** 1845)

77. The adult male great frigatebird, **Fregata minor,** displays a bright red throat sac during mating season, as seen here on Tower Island.

78. Female great frigatebird, **Fregata minor,** with chick on Tower Island.

79. Male great frigatebird displaying courtship posture on Tower Island. To attract mates the males spread their wings and throw back their heads showing off their bright red throat sac. At the same time they make eerie warbling sounds.

80. There are about 500 greater flamingos, **Phoenicopterus ruber,** found in salty lagoons around the archipelago. The most common place for visitors to view them is the lagoon at Punta Cormorant, Floreana Island. They feed by filtering out of the bottom mud, shrimp and other small marine animals.

81. A greater flamingo spreads its wings, displaying its elegant plumage.

82. The endemic lava gull, **Larus fuliginosus,** is thought to be the rarest in the world, with only some 400 mating pairs in existence.

83. Brown pelicans, **Pelecanus occidentalis,** are plentiful around most anchorages, waiting for scraps to be thrown overboard from ships' galleys.

84. The endemic flightless cormorant, **Nannopterum harrisi,** has traded flight for a streamlined swimming body. Upon leaving the water, it assumes the classic wing-drying stance shown here at Punta Espinosa, Fernandina Island.

85. The yellow-crowned night heron, **Nyctanassa violacea,** normally feeds at night, and can be found during day in the shade of shoreline cliffs and rocks.

86. The American oystercatcher, **Haematopus ostralegus,** is found mainly along rocky shores where it searches for intertidal creatures. The population in Galapagos is small, with only some 150 pairs. In the photograph it is seen in its classic one-legged stance. In the foreground is a Sally lightfoot crab, **Grapsus grapsus.**

87. Great blue herons, **Ardea herodias,** can be found throughout the archipelago. They are commonly seen around shorelines and mangroves where they hunt for fish. Occasionally, they also feed on newly hatched turtles and marine iguanas. Here, one dries its wings at Punta Espinosa, Fernandina Island.

88. A great blue heron in its classic one-legged stance at Punta Espinosa, Fernandina Island.

89. The endemic Galapagos dove, **Nesopelia galapagoensis,** is an especially attractive bird. In the past their numbers were greatly reduced by hunting, and much of their reported tameness has been lost.

90. The Galapagos mockingbird, **Nesomimus parvulus,** is one of four endemic species found in the archipelago. Inquisitive and relatively tame, these birds are often the first to greet visitors upon arriving at landing areas. This photograph was taken on Tower Island.

PLANTS

PLANTS

Plants have always been a source of fascination on the islands of Galapagos. As Charles Darwin observed, though many species were closely related to those found on mainland South America, a surprising number were unique to Galapagos - endemic, that is. For example, Darwin collected 71 legumes on Santiago (James) and, of these, 38 were confined to Galapagos. An even more stunning fact was that 30 of the 38 were found only on Santiago. Further studies by botanists confirmed these observations. Today it is generally accepted that 34 percent of the plant species are endemic and, if subspecies and varieties (collectively called taxa) are considered, the figure jumps to 42 percent - and indeed, many of the taxa have evolved on only one island. These observations had a great influence on Darwin's work, and today continue to intrigue visitors who take the time to learn about them.

An excellent example of plant divergence is displayed by the genus *Scalesia*. *Scalesia* is to the flora of Galapagos what "Darwin's Finches" are to the fauna. Members of the sunflower-daisy family, this endemic genus has evolved into some 20 separate taxa. Almost half of the taxa are found on only one island. They are also, generally, separated by environmental zones. The superficial appearance of many of these plants is so radically different that it is difficult for most people to believe they are from the same genus.

Four examples of *Scalesia* clearly illustrate this great divergence in appearance. *S. villosa*, found in the arid zone of Floreana, is a low shrub with hairy, long, narrow leaves that produces large flowers. *S. helleri*, found in the arid zone of Santa Fe, is a low shrub with highly divided leaves that produces a large flower. *S. cordata*, found in the arid zone of Isabela, grows to be a small tree, up to ten meters high, with heart-shaped leaves, that produces a small flower. *S. pedunculata*, found in the moist highlands of Santa Cruz, Floreana, San Cristobal and Santiago, is a large tree that grows up to 20 meters high with thin, elongated, pear-shaped leaves, which produces a small flower. Yet, all these radically different appearing plants are of the same heritage and genus.

For many visitors, the most striking plant in Galapagos is the giant prickly pear tree. This member of the Cactus family, classified in the genus *Opuntia*, has evolved into 14 endemic taxa. Unlike *Scalesia*, however, the close relationship between members of the genus is obvious - all grow large, round, green, well-spined pads. Divergence between taxa ranges from low shrubby forms to giant trees, which on Santa Cruz may reach 12 meters in height. The juicy pads are a favorite food of land iguanas and tortoises. Interestingly, the tree forms tend to grow on islands where these animals were present. This fact leads to speculation that the cactus tree trunks evolved as a response to iguana and tortoise feeding habits.

Cactus are a dominant flora in many island areas. The commonly seen genera, *Jasminocereus* and *Brachycereus*, are both endemic to the Archipelago. Lava cactus, *B. nesioticus*, also endemic, is one of the first plants to inhabit new lava flows. It is an attractive little cactus that grows in clumps of small, unbranched, dome-topped cylinders. New growth is yellow in color which, with age, turns orange and then dark grayish-green. Like great organ pipes, the stately candelabra cactus, *J. thouarsii*, towers to seven meters. Hundreds can be seen on the rocky hillsides. Often they spring up from lava flows where there appears to be no soil to which they can attach.

The most common tree in Galapagos is the Palo Santo, *Bursera graveolens*, which thrives in arid regions. It is a relative of frankincense and myrrh and, when burned, produces a fragrant smoke that repels insects. The common name, Palo Santo, means "holy stick." There are two theories for the origin of the name: one from its use as incense in South American churches; the other is from its habit of coming to leaf and flower around Christmas time. In the dry season, its leafless, pale gray branches form intriguing line designs against the demonic red volcanic material in the background. The bark's pale gray comes from a covering of crustose lichens which mask its true purplish color.

One of the most colorful plants in Galapagos is *Sesuvium*. It is a fleshy, ground-covering plant that land iguanas graze upon. Its color changes from green in the wet season, to yellow and finally bright red near the end of the dry season. There is no more dramatic landscape in Galapagos than South Plaza Island when covered with crimson mats of endemic *Sesuvium*, punctuated by stands of prickly pear trees. Near sunset, the cactus spines glow in the last direct rays of sunlight, outlining the trees in gold.

The gray mat plant, *Tiquilia spp.*, is another arid zone survivor. Four endemic species inhabit sandy and ash-covered areas. Often, as on the slopes of Bartolome, it is the only plant found. Another sand-dweller is the beach morning glory, *Ipomoea pes-caprae*. This creeping vine is important in stabilizing the sandy shoreline. Its funnel-shaped, mauve colored flowers are among the largest found in Galapagos, and add wonderful splashes of color to beach edge areas.

The island highlands of Santa Cruz, San Cristobal, Isabela and Santiago often lay covered in clouds. This moisture transforms them into lush, tropical zones. For example, on Santa Cruz there are forests dominated by *Scalesia pedunculata*. These trees are festooned with mosses, liverworts, ferns, orchids and bromeliads. There are over 90 species of ferns, including the beautiful fern-tree, *Cyathea weatherbyana*, that grows to over three meters in height. In some locations the ground covering of ferns is so thick that it becomes difficult to walk. These highland areas offer an interesting and refreshing contrast to the sparse vegetation of the arid zones that typify the islands.

91

92

95

96

97

98

100

101

102

104

105

106

107

108

109

110

111

112

113

114

115

80

PLANTS
PICTURE CAPTIONS

91. Endemic prickly pear cactus, **Opuntia** spp., have evolved into 14 types, including this tree seen on South Plaza Island.

92. The spines of prickly pear trees glow in the late afternoon sun on South Plaza Island. The ground is matted with endemic **Sesuvium edmonstonei**.

93. The endemic prickly pear cactus tree is thought, by some, to have evolved its protective trunk as a response to the tortoises which fed on its juicy lower pads.

94. Majestic stands of endemic candelabra cactus, **Jasminocereus thouarsii**, are often be seen on lava fields where there appears to be nothing to support their roots.

95. Detail of endemic lava cactus, **Brachycereus nesioticus**.

96. Lava cactus is often the only plant visible on young lava flows. A good example is this clump on the lava flow at Punta Espinosa, Fernandina Island.

97. Endemic gray mat plant, **Tiquilia nesiotica**, is one of the few plants found on ash-covered ground.

98. Gray mat plant abounds on the ash-covered slopes of Bartholome Island. Pinnacle rock can be seen in the distance.

99. The velvet daisy, **Scalesia villosa**, is a species endemic to Floreana Island. It can be found along the park trail to the flamingo lagoon at Punta Cormorant.

100. The cut leaf daisy, **Lecocarpus pinnatifidus**, is also endemic to Floreana Island. It can be seen growing from beds of volcanic cinders along the park trail to the flamingo lagoon at Punta Cormorant.

101. Morning glories produce some of the largest blossoms in the archipelago. Seen on Tower Island is the endemic lava morning glory, **Ipomoea habeliona**.

102. Wine-colored centers characterize the endemic morning glory, **Ipomoea linearifola**, photographed on the slopes of Daphne Major.

103. Beach morning glories, **Ipomoea pes-caprae**, are important in stabilizing sand along beachfronts, as seen here at Villamil Beach, Isabela Island.

104.-105. Palo santo or "holy stick" trees, **Bursera graveolens**, produce a fragrant smoke when burned and are often used as incense in churches on the mainland. They are among the most common trees in the archipelago. During the dry season they are gaunt and leafless. Their pale, gray colored bark stands out against the volcanic rock background in fascinating patterns created by the branches. During rainy periods, leaves and small fragrant flowers appear, transforming the scene completely. The contrast between the two seasons is dramatically displayed in these two pictures taken above Tagus Cove, Isabela Island.

106. The bark of palo santo trees gets its color from a covering of crustose lichens. The purple-tinged bark's true color can usually be seen near shore where the salt atmosphere hinders the lichens' growth.

107. Endemic **Sesuvium, Sesuvium edmonstonei**, turns bright red near the end of the dry season.

108. South Plaza Island is ablaze with mats of **Sesuvium**.

109. Mangroves, the pioneer shrubs and trees found along sheltered coasts and on the fringes of lagoons, are seen here at Punta Espinosa, Fernandina Island.

110. The highlands of the four major islands are often cloud covered, and thus receive more moisture than the rest of the archipelago. Only in these highlands does one find the lush tropical growth that is associated with the equatorial regions of the South American mainland. A pit crater in the highlands of Santa Cruz Island is surrounded by thick vegetation.

111. The highland areas of Santa Cruz support what are known as **Scalesia** forests. Most are surprised to learn that these large trees, **Scalesia pedunculata**, are members of the daisy-sunflower family. They are festooned with lichens, liverworts, mosses and bromeliads.

112. A young fern branch, just beginning to open in the highlands of Santa Cruz Island.

113. Many species of ferns are abundant in the tortoise reserve on Santa Cruz Island. The ferns seen in this photograph are **Asplenium auritum**.

114. The leaf of **Doryopteris pedata** has an unusual shape for a fern.

115. This beautiful design of nature is formed by endemic Darwin's aster, **Darwiniothamnus tenuifolius var. tenuifolius**, common to the highlands of Santa Cruz Island.

MARINE MAMMALS
AND OTHER SUBJECTS

MARINE MAMMALS
AND OTHER SUBJECTS

The most notable marine mammals in the archipelago are the Galapagos sea lions, *Zalophus californianus wollebacki*. Their anthropomorphic behavior captivates the imagination of virtually every visitor. They are inquisitive, playful and, at times, lazy. It is estimated that there are over 50,000 individuals in the islands. Visitors are introduced to them almost immediately as they frolic around the small shore excursion boats (pangas). Once ashore, there is no more endearing sight than a group of sea lions lazily soaking up the sun on the beach.

Their inquisitiveness can become almost pesky. On more than one occasion while working underwater, I have felt the presence of something or someone and turned to find a sea lion looking over my shoulder to see what I was doing. This playfulness is often unnerving. Occasionally they will come out of the blue void at full speed, streaking past your face plate like screaming jet fighters on a bombing run. Your natural reflexes cause a panicked duck before your conscious mind comprehends that it is only a cavorting sea lion. At times these capers can become quite irritating. Several years ago while I was exploring a 50-foot sand bottom near Espanola (Hood), I came upon a red lipped batfish, *Ogcocephalus darwini*, the first I had ever seen.

Carefully I maneuvered into position for a picture, but before I could snap the shutter a blur shot in front of the camera lens. I looked up to see that a sea lion had playfully picked up the batfish and was zooming for the surface. I could not believe what had happened. Then, much to my surprise, the batfish came floating down from above, settling right in front of me. Amazingly, it appeared no worse for the wear. I set up for another picture and again, before I could take it, the sea lion took off with my batfish. Repeat performances of these episodes continued until I gave up in disgust.

Fur seals, *Arctocephalus galapagoensis*, an endemic species, are seen less often because they prefer rocky, rugged, shaded shore areas. The common name, seals, is a misnomer, as they are really a type of sea lion. They are smaller than the Galapagos sea lions, and have a thick fur coat. Much prized by furriers in the 19th and early 20th centuries, they were almost hunted to extinction. Since a ban on hunting, however, they have made a remarkable comeback. Their population now nears 50,000. A good place to view these delightful animals, both above and below the water, is the fur seal grotto at James Bay on Santiago.

Dolphins, which have always captured the imagination of man, are plentiful in the waters of Galapagos. Hardly a visitor leaves without seeing them jump and play. Three species are common. Bottle-nosed dolphins, *Tursiops truncatus*, love to frolic in front of a running boat's bow. They will ride the bow wave and then, as if playing tag, touch the bow with their tails. When breaching the water for air, they will occasionally make spectacular full-bodied leaps from the sea. Spinner dolphins, *Stenella longirostris*, and common dolphins, *Delphinus delphis*, are less likely to be seen near boats. When spotted however, they are often in great schools of a hundred or more, jumping and tumbling in the distance.

Although the bottle-nosed dolphins seem to enjoy the company of human beings while they are aboard a ship, they shy away from scuba divers. Their behavior toward groups of snorkelers is much the same; however, with only a few people in the water, they sometimes come around. On one occasion, off Roca Redonda, we stopped our boat to try our luck with a group that had been playing around the ship. To our pleasant surprise, it was one of those special times when they wanted to play. They seemed attracted to our clumsy attempts at surface diving and would swim over for a closer look. The interaction was short-lived, however, as they soon departed.

Every nature lover is thrilled with the sight of a whale. Since whaling has ceased around the islands, their populations seem to be returning. Sightings, although still not common, are no longer considered rare. Whale populations around Galapagos include the finback, sei, humpback, minke, pilot and sperm. The large sperm whales, *Physeter macrocephalus*, are an elusive group about which little is known. They were made famous as fearsome creatures in Herman Melville's MOBY DICK.

Only a few underwater pictures of them have ever been taken. Recently, while working on a television special, I had a two week opportunity to try and capture these leviathans on film. Photographing a 40-to 60-foot animal underwater, in the open ocean, is no easy feat and considered dangerous by many. First, you must have the good fortune of finding the animals; then catch them at rest on the surface; and, finally, have water clear enough to see the entire animal - something in excess of 100-foot visibility is needed. Thirteen of our 14 days were filled with frustration as we often had two, but not all three, of the requirements. Sperm whales have an unusual social behavior of occasionally joining together in a rafting behavior while resting on the surface in the late afternoon. On one occasion, we had over 50 whales raft next to our boat - an unbelievable, once-in-a-lifetime, photographic opportunity that was foiled by 15-foot visibility!

Late one afternoon all of the conditions were right and I slipped into the water close to a pair of whales. The swim toward them seemed to take forever. I now realize, in retrospect, that I was fooled by their immense size and mistakenly thought I was closer when I entered the water. My first view of the giants was awesome - in front of me was a mother and calf bathed in the electric blue rays of afternoon sun. I was transfixed - all I could do was stare. Then the mother moved in my direction while showering me with a barrage of sonar clicks. Within camera range she hesitated, then sounded into the blue void below. Before following its mother, the apparently playful calf performed several barrel rolls (a previously unrecorded behavior) and then dived into the deep. This brief experience in the presence of such magnificent creatures will always be cherished.

116

119

120

121

122

123

124

125

127

128

129

131

132

133

92

134

135

136

137

138

139

96

MARINE MAMMALS AND OTHER SUBJECTS
PICTURE CAPTIONS

*116. Bottle-nosed dolphins, **Tursiops truncatus**, are often observed playing alongside the bows of a moving ships. Occasionally they make spectacular leaps into the air.*

117. Bottle-nosed dolphins normally leave the area when divers enter the water, but on occasion will allow snorkelers to approach them.

*118. Unlike the bottle-nosed dolphins, spinner dolphins, **Stenella longirostris**, are much less likely to swim around ships. When they are observed, however, the sight is usually thrilling as they often travel in schools of over 100.*

*119. Sperm whales, **Physeter macrocephalus**, are occasionally observed around the archipelago, especially off the western sides of Isabela and Fernandina Islands. These mammoth cetaceans raise their flukes in an impressive display when sounding.*

120. Sperm whales, for unknown reasons, occasionally breach high into the air and then fall back into the water with resounding splashes.

121. Once in awhile, in the late afternoon, sperm whales are observed rafting together on the surface, a mysterious social behavior. On the occasion that this photograph was taken, over 40 whales were present.

122.-123. Rare underwater photographs of a sperm whale sounding.

*124. The Galapagos sea lion, **Zalophus californianus wollebacki**, is a subspecies of the California sea lion, its smaller size being the primary difference between the two.*

125. Galapagos sea lions lazily sunning and snoozing at the landing on South Plaza Island.

126. Sea lions playfully frolic and cavort around landing parties, captivating the attention of virtually every visitor.

127. The large doe-like eyes of sea lions endear them to all visitors. Very inquisitive, they often approach divers to investigate the strange intruders into their marine environment.

*128. Sea lions playing underwater in a bed of endemic, yellow-black coral, **Antipathes galapagensis**.*

129. A sea lion kicks up clouds of white sand while performing playful "aquabatics" for a diver.

130. Young sea lions tirelessly play together underwater.

131. Sea lions at sunset. Daphne Minor is in the background.

132. Rope-like surface flows of lava are called "pahoehoe," which is a Polynesian term for "ropey."

133. The huge lava flow of pahoehoe, seen at Sullivan Bay on Santiago Island, is an amazing display of the fascinating patterns and shapes that molten rock can form. Pinnacle rock can be seen in the background.

134. Pahoehoe flows produce an endless maze of engrossing designs.

135. A brilliant splash of color and design characterize the caterpillar form of the sphinx moth.

*136. Sally lightfoot crabs, **Grapsus grapsus**, are the most dazzling colored animals found above water in Galapagos. They get their name from their ability to skip across the water's surface for short distances, as if "walking on water." Their brilliant colors are but a hint of the beauty to be found beneath the sea's surface.*

*137.-138.-139. One of the most resplendent displays of color found underwater comes from the extended polyps of an endemic cup coral, **Tubastraea tagusensis**. It was found primarily along the west coast of Isabela and around Fernandina. One of the most notable locations to view this coral was on the walls of Tagus Cove. At night, the splashes of color were so profuse that the wall resembled a giant painter's palette. Regrettably, the 1982-83 "El Niño," the most severe on record, raised water temperatures so high that these wondrous colonies of coral died. At the time of this writing, no living colonies of this coral have been reported since the "El Niño", indicating the species may have become extinct. (An "El Niño" is a climatic condition that occasionally affects the archipelago. It is characterized by a flow of warm water and increased rainfall.)*

FISH

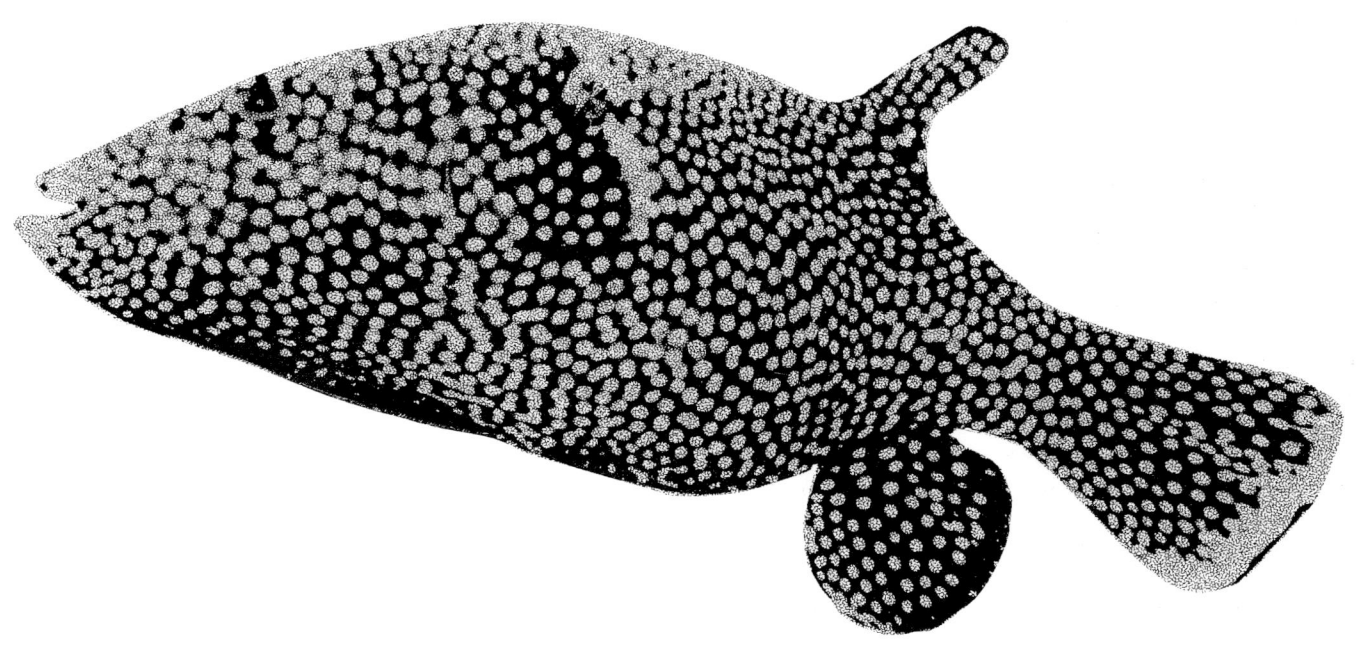

FISH

The waters surrounding the Galapagos archipelago are a mixture of cold antarctic currents from the south and warmer tropical currents from equatorial flows. This mixture of waters has brought an unusual collection of fish to the region. Here you will find brightly colored, tropical, coral reef fish such as the moorish idol, tiger snake eel, coral and long-nose hawkfish swimming with such typically cold water species as the Peruvian grunt and Pacific red sheephead. Nearly 20 percent of the 300-plus species of fish found in the islands are endemic. Several species, such as the Galapagos shark, *Carcharhinus galapagensis*, and red-lipped batfish, *Ogcocephalus darwini*, were first thought to be endemic to Galapagean waters. However, they have since been seen in other waters and, thus, are only indigenous. Because the currents that sweep into the archipelago are rich in nutrients, fish life abounds. Great fish schools are seen on virtually every dive. This unique abundance of fish life is why Galapagos is a "world-class" diving destination.

Sharks spark the imagination. Regrettably, the most common perception is that all shark encounters are hair-raising experiences. In Galapagos, these fears are reinforced when boat crews clean fresh fish and throw the remains overboard. Sharks, attracted by the scent of fish blood, hungrily snap up the remains. I've heard more than one visitor, upon viewing this spectacle, exclaim that anyone would be crazy to enter these "shark-infested" waters!

Galapagos waters do have a high concentration of sharks. Few diving visitors leave without sighting several of these sleek dynamos. The problem, however, is not the danger; instead, it is getting near enough to closely observe and photograph them. The sharks of Galapagos are quite shy around divers and it takes some work, skill and a lot of luck to get within a reasonable distance. Non-divers may well wonder why one would want to get close to these efficient "killing machines." The reason is that to observe these magnificent creatures in their natural environment is a thrill that can hardly be matched. Unquestionably, it is one of the most beautiful displays in the Animal Kingdom of graceful power in motion. One comforting bit of information; there has never been a reported shark attack on a diver in the archipelago.

Peter Benchley, author of JAWS, was the host of a television special about the marine life of Galapagos. I was his companion and guide. Naturally, it was incumbent upon us to shoot some footage of divers with Galapagos sharks. Roca Redonda, an isolated rock outcropping northwest of the major islands, has always produced good shark action, so that is where we headed for the filming. The Galapagos shark is a "classic," the clean sharp head, trim body and great scythe tail appear to be sculptured from silver. When we dropped into the water on our first dive, there were three sharks directly below us. However, as we descended, they gracefully turned and swam from view. During the balance of the dive we saw a few more sharks, but they, too, kept their distance - well out of camera range. The next two days of diving, to our disappointment, were much the same. We had to be content with filming great schools of rainbow runners, amber jacks, yellow-tailed grunts, crevalle jacks, barracuda and yellow-striped snappers that were moving through the area. This at least kept us busy as we searched for the elusive predators.

The third day was different - as we reached the bottom there were sharks all around. Often we could see two dozen sharks at once! Several made slow, cautious approaches and we began to film. There is no explanation for this change in behavior, but as the dive wore on, the passes, although still apparently unthreatening, kept getting closer and closer. Toward the end of the dive they were coming to within a few feet - close enough to make the hair on your neck stand. Peter indicated that he had had enough - I agreed. Our hearts were still pumping hard from the excitement as we surfaced.

There are many exotic reef fish in the waters of the archipelago. The moorish idol, *Zanclus cornutus*, looks like something from a Picasso painting. It has a trumpet-like snout with orange triangular markings. The body is round and thin with a tall sweeping dorsal fin and forked tail. Distinct black, white and yellow lines band the body. The king angle fish, *Holocanthus passer*, has a deep blue body which is distinguished by orange markings on the fins and head, a pure white band just behind the gill plate and a brilliant yellow tail. The longnose hawkfish, *Oxycirrhites typus*, has a white body with a blood-red line design of squares on its sides. This cute little fish can be found hiding in the branches of yellow black coral. The list of reef fish goes on and on, enough to keep any fish-watcher happy, dive after dive.

One of the most majestic fish in Galapagean waters is the leopard spotted eagle ray, *Aetobatus narinari*. Often these long-tailed rays will "fly" in graceful formations through open water. They have always been difficult to approach and photograph, and will bolt away if chased. My most successful ploy, which works only rarely, is to swim slowly into a position directly in their line of travel, then stay as motionless as possible, hoping they will fly to you.

Once, I had carefully maneuvered into such a position and the rays were coming straight to me. I was on the verge of snapping pictures, when suddenly I was enveloped in a huge swirling school of silver amberjacks! I was livid, after working so hard to get into a favorable position - then to be thwarted by this school of relatively common fish. Luck, however, was on my side. The jacks parted just in time to perfectly frame two of the rays, producing one of my favorite photographs.

140

142

143

144

145

100

147

148

149

150

151

152

153

155

154

156

157

158

108

159

160

161

162

163

164

165

166

167

168

FISH
PICTURE CAPTIONS

140. Large fine-spotted moray eels, **Gymnothorax dovii** (approx. 4ft.), are common in the waters of Galapagos. These sinister looking fish are, in reality, quite timid animals that normally retreat upon a diver's approach. The menacing display of their sharp, teeth-filled mouths, constantly opening and closing, is merely an action required to pump water through their gills for respiration.

141. Scalloped hammerhead sharks, **Sphyrna lewini** (approx. 10ft.), rarely menace divers, but instead normally retreat upon their approach.

142. Port Jackson horn sharks, **Heterodontus quoyi** (approx. 3ft.), are nocturnal creatures that usually rest on the bottom during daylight hours.

143. Galapagos sharks, **Carcharhinus galapagensis** (approx. 7½ft.), were originally thought to be endemic to the archipelago; however, they have since been reported elsewhere. Generally, these sharks are timid around divers, but have been known to make close, inquisitive approaches.

144.-145. The Guineafowl puffer, **Arothron meleagris** (approx. 9in.), is generally black bodied with white spots, but occasionally displays a brilliant golden color phase.

146. One of the most thrilling sights in the Galapagean seascape is a formation of majestic eagle rays, **Aetobatus narinari** (approx. 6ft.), "flying" through the water.

147.-148. The king angelfish, **Holocanthus passer** (approx. 7in.), is the only large angelfish found in the waters of Galapagos. It is abundant and often seen in large schools foraging about shallow reefs. Below is the brilliant red Pacific creolefish, **Paranthias colonus**, normally seen in large schools on all reefs in Galapagos. The juvenile king angelfish is more brightly colored than the adult, with a golden body and bright blue vertical stripes.

149. Steel pompano, **Trachinotus stilbe** (approx. 9in.), feed in large schools, near the surface, throughout the archipelago.

150. The bravo clinid, **Labrisomus dentriticus** (approx. 6in.), is an odd looking fish that rests on its pectoral fins in calm, sandy areas.

151. Juvenile leather bass, **Epinephelus dermatolepis** (approx. 4in.), have black and white stripes that blend well with the long spines of sea urchins. They have the amazing ability of swimming among the sharp, dangerous spines, using them for protective shelter.

152.-153. The Pacific spotted scorpionfish, **Scorpaena mystes** (approx. 12in.), has venomous spines in its dorsal fin. Its ability to change color enables it to become almost indistinguishable from the background. Camouflage is further enhanced by skin flaps called barbels which resemble algae. They sit quietly on the bottom, waiting for unsuspecting prey to come within close range.

154. Schooling amberjacks, **Seriola rivoliana** (approx. 3 ft.), almost block the view of majestic eagle rays, **Aetobatus narinari**.

155. Moorish Idols, **Zanclus cornutus** (approx. 8in.), are one of the tropical Indo-Pacific fish found in the cool waters of Galapagos. These colorful, shallow water reef fish look as if they were designed by Pablo Picasso.

156. The Pacific seahorse, **Hippocampus ingens** (approx. 6in.), although not common, is found in Galapagean waters. These relatively large seahorses are often spotted, and are highly variable in color. They may be red, black, light brown or gold and are often found hiding in the branches of golden seafans, **Muricea** sp., or black coral, **Antipathes** spp.

157. The redtail triggerfish, **Xanthichthys mento** (approx. 9in.), are occasionally seen in the northernmost waters of the archipelago.

158. Porcupine fish, **Diodon hystrix** (approx. 15in.), protect themselves from predators by rapidly inflating their bodies and extending their long, sharp spines.

159.-160. The endemic barnacle blenny, **Acanthemblemaria castroi** (approx. 2½in.), often inhabits empty barnacle shells as well as other cracks and crevices. They will sit in the shells, with only their heads in view, waiting for food to float by. When it does, they dart quickly from the security of their shells to grab it.

161. The endemic Galapagos pufferfish, **Sphoeroides angusticeps** (approx. 8in.), has beautiful, opal-like eyes and is seen here swimming over pebble coral, **Cycloseris mexicana**.

162. Although it has striking colors, the sanguine frogfish, **Antennarius sanguineus** (approx. 4in.), blends well with the background, making it almost indistinguishable to predators and prey alike.

163. A bizarre pattern of lines and bars is the trademark of the hieroglyphic hawkfish, **Cirrhitus rivulatus** (approx. 1ft.). This unusually large hawkfish can grow up to 20 inches.

164. The wrasse-assed bass, **Liopropoma fasciatum** (approx. 1ft.), is a brightly colored, inquisitive fish that will come out of hiding to investigate a diver.

165. The tiny blue banded goby, **Lythrypnus gilberti** (approx. 1in.), is a beautiful endemic species that is plentiful throughout the archipelago.

166. Female Mexican hogfish, **Bodianus diplotaenia** (approx. 1ft.), displaying "kissing" behavior, which is actually a form of fighting.

167. The longnose hawkfish, **Oxycirrhites typus** (approx. 3in.), can often be found hiding in the branches of yellow-black coral. Like other hawkfish, they rest on their pectoral fins.

168. A coral hawkfish, **Cirrhitichthys oxycephalus** (approx. 3in), sits in the rust colored branches of bushy black coral, **Antipathes** sp. Both the longnose and coral hawkfish are good examples of brightly colored, tropical reef fish that inhabit the cool waters of Galapagos along with cold-water species, as both species are found throughout the tropical Indo-Pacific.

MARINE INVERTEBRATES

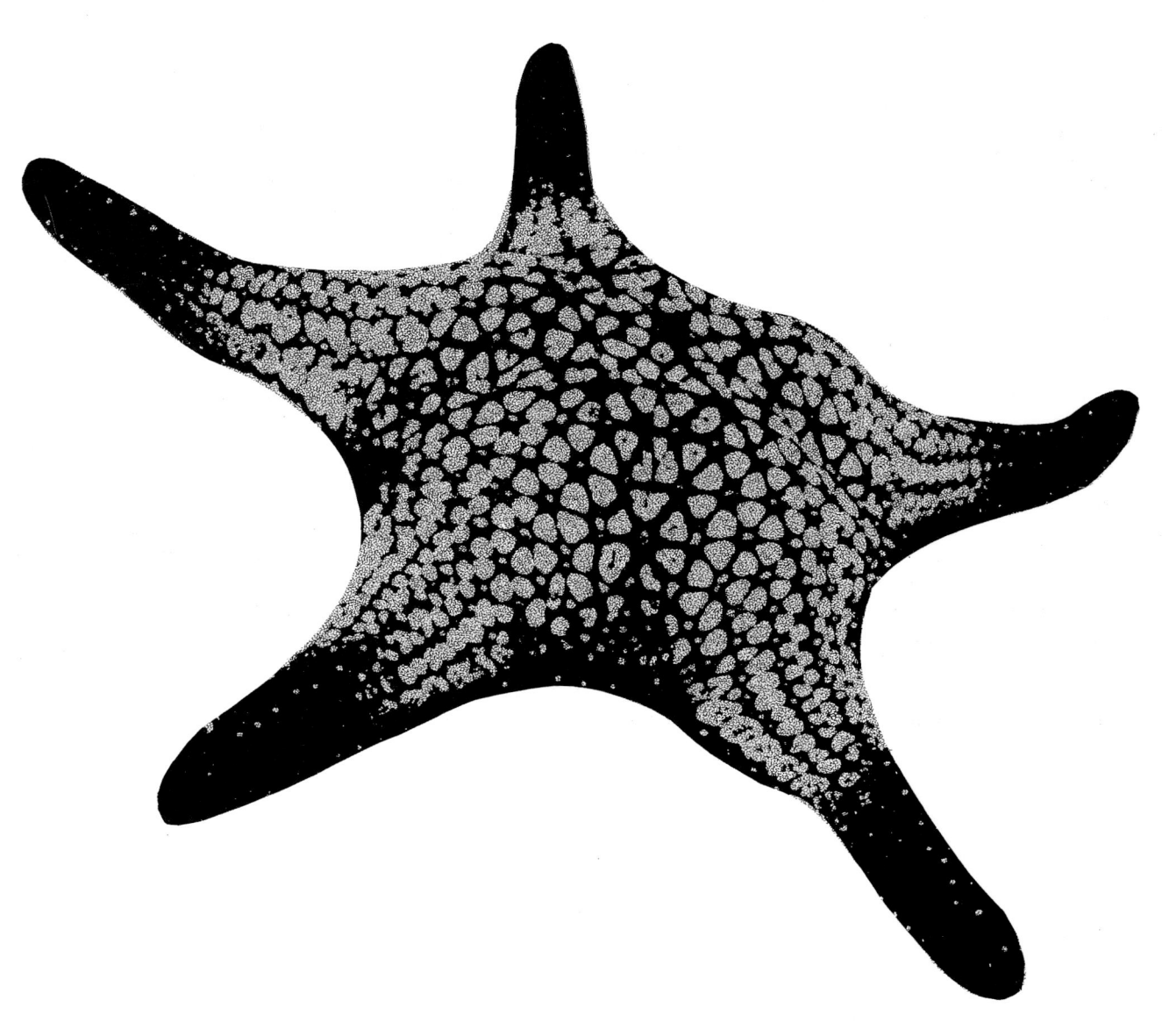

MARINE INVERTEBRATES

The marine invertebrates found in Galapagos are a colorful lot, adding daring splashes of color to a drab substrate of volcanic origin. The average temperature of the waters around the archipelago is too cold to support most reef-building corals. Only in shallow waters, where the sun keeps the water temperature above normal, do these corals struggle to exist. However, a beautiful non-reef-building hard coral, called orange cup coral, *Tubastraea coccinea*, is abundant. Found in shaded areas of the reef, its hues of yellow, orange and pink form exquisite designs on the lava rock substrate. When its polyps are extended, the colonies look like wondrous floral displays.

Great bushes of yellow-black coral, *Antipathes galapagensis*, also add resplendent splashes of color to the reef. There are some areas in Galapagos where the bottom is covered with great boulders of volcanic stone. The yellow-black coral is so profuse that it looks like a rock garden in the spring, with yellow/chartreuse flowering shrubbery. The name is not a contradiction in terms, as this endemic black coral gets its name from the yellow/chartreuse colored pigment found in its flesh. The underlying skeletal structure is indeed black, as are all black corals, but this is not apparent until the coral dies. Unlike some of its famous relatives, however, it is not of gem quality, a trait that may well have kept it from serious depletion by unthinking people who harvest this rare and slow-growing coral.

Another colorful addition to the reefs are large sea fans, *Muricea sp.*, whose extended polyps are brilliant gold. I know of several places in Galapagos where underwater cliff faces are covered with these majestic fans, making a swim through their outstretched arms a trip into fantasy land. Thanks primarily to these marine invertebrates, Galapagos' reefs are far from the drab, colorless environment one might expect.

Starfish are abundant and add a kaleidoscope of colors and patterns to the reefs. The most common are gulf stars, *Oreaster occidentalis*, with distinctive, bright red spines. They are often decorated with a beautiful red and white geometric design. The purple, spotted star, *Phataria unifascialis*, is often found foraging about on bottoms of coral and barnacle shell rubble. Spined blood stars, *Astropecten sp.*, are a brilliant red and can be found on sand bottoms where they often bury themselves during the day. One of the most unique appearing starfish in Galapagean waters is the sunstar, *Heliaster multiradiata*. This multi-armed echinoderm tucks its legs under its body during the day, losing its typical starfish appearance. Instead, it looks like a fist sized black dome covered with short red or yellow spines. The list of starfish species found here seems endless.

For me, the most beautiful marine invertebrate on the reefs is the magnificent scallop shell, *Pecten magnificens*. Its fluted shells are about 15 centimeters in diameter and, when they open, a crimson mantel is revealed. On this red background are patches of shimmering violet and bright blue eye spots. Its edges are fringed with golden yellow tentacles. The trick to photographing these animals is to catch them with their shells open, mantel exposed. Timid of a diver's approach, they normally snap their shells shut. You are then left to play a quiet waiting game, hoping the animal will regain confidence and open its shells, revealing the wondrous beauty inside. Once I had been waiting a long time before the shells finally started to open. I was prepared to take my first picture when suddenly they snapped shut again and I felt a gentle tug on my strobe arm. I turned in anger toward the inconsiderate diver who had frightened my subject. But there was no diver; instead, it was a playful sea lion with his mouth around my strobe. Sea lion antics such as this are just one of the pleasurable things you have to put up with in Galapagos waters.

Another resplendent addition to the reef is the golden-snouted shrimp, *Rhynchocinetes sp.* Found primarily along the west coast of Isabela and around Fernandina, these bright red crustaceans can be found inhabiting cracks, crevices, and other small dark recesses in the reef. Shy creatures, they normally retreat and hide from view when divers approach. After a short wait, however, they become curious and cautiously come out of hiding. Once, while I was observing a magnificent scallop, I rested my hand near one of their dark hiding places. Shortly thereafter, I felt a strange tingling sensation on my hand. I looked down and, much to my surprise saw about four shrimp gently picking at my flesh in a cleaning behavior. It was definitely the strangest manicure I've ever had.

Virtually every class of marine invertebrate is represented in Galapagos, many of them endemic. There are feather-like hydroids, colorful nudibranchs, prehistoric appearing slipper lobsters, crabs and hermit crabs, Christmas tree worms, flat worms, feather duster worms, anemones, sea urchins, sea cucumbers, sand dollars, tunicates, snails, scallops, clams and oysters; an exhaustless reserve of beauty and intrigue.

170

171

172

173

174

175

176

177

178

179

180

181

182

183

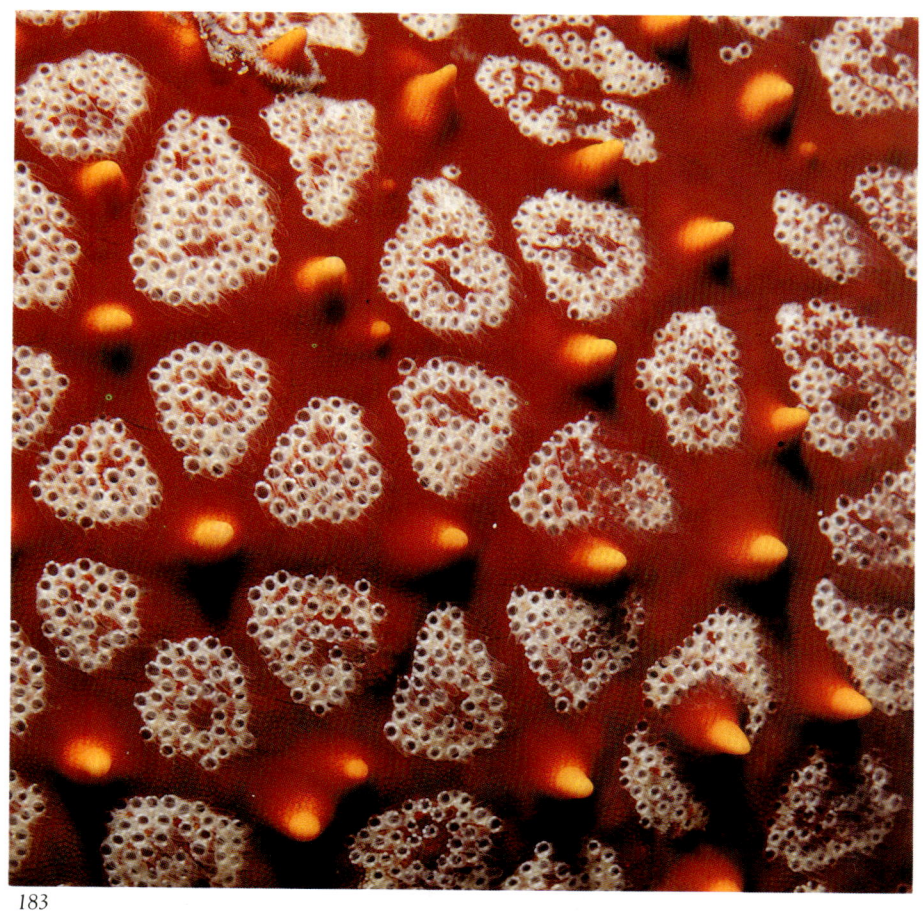
184

123

185

186

187

188

189

190

191

192

193

128

MARINE INVERTEBRATES

PICTURE CAPTIONS

169. Orange cup coral, **Tubastraea coccinea** (extended polyp, approx. ½in.), is an abundant non-reef-building coral found throughout the archipelago. Its extended polyps are an intense orange that forms beautiful floral-like displays on mundane volcanic walls.

170. Leopard spotted anemones, **Antiparactis** sp. (extended polyp, approx. 1in.), are attractive whether the polyps are open or closed. This animal feeds by catching food in its open tentacles, which are used bring the food to its mouth at the center of the oral disc. The tentacles have tiny stinging cells called nematocysts, which help immobilize prey.

171. Detail of a golden sea fan, **Muricea** sp. (extended polyp, approx. ⅛in.), that grows in profusion on some reefs in the archipelago. The fans are not plants as many suspect. They are, in fact, a colony composed of thousands of tiny individual animals called polyps, each having eight tentacles, as seen in this photograph.

172. Zoanthids, **Zoanthus** sp. (extended polyp, approx. ¼in), are small animal polyps that are closely related to sea anemones. These colored polyps grow in profusion on rocks just below water level. They can be found throughout the archipelago, but are especially abundant on the west coast of Isabela Island, and around Fernandina Island.

173. Growth pattern detail of a true-reef building hard coral, **Gardineroseris planulata**, found in shallow reef areas.

174. A large, red banded, hairy hermit crab, **Aniculus elegans**, uses an empty shell as a home.

175. Swimming crab, **Cronius ruber** (approx. 8in.).

176. This unidentified flatworm, of the **Phylum Platyhelminthes** (approx. 2½in.), Order Polycladida, was found off Punta Vicente Roca on Isabela Island.

177. Octopus are common on the reefs in Galapagos, but are rarely observed by divers because of their nocturnal feeding habits and their amazing ability to change color to blend with almost any background. Note how the octopus in the photograph is difficult to distinguish, except for one arm which, for unknown reasons, is an intense blue.

178. Yellow-snouted red shrimp, **Rhynchocinetes** sp. (approx. 2in.), are profuse along the west coast of Isabela Island and around Fernandina Island. These are cleaner shrimp and feed by cleaning fish of parasites and food debris. At first they are shy of a diver's approach, but with slow, unthreatening movements they will come out to feed by cleaning a diver's fingers and hand much as they would clean a fish!

179. These beautiful, feather-like branches are of an animal colony called feather hydroids, **Lytocarpus** sp.. The branches are actually built by thousands of microscopic animal polyps whose stinging nematocyst cells can inflict a painful sting.

180. Nudibranchs are members of the snail family **Gastropoda** (approx. 1in.) who have lost their shells. Their bodies are often brightly colored and ornate in design. At the head is a pair of sensory antennae and, in some species, further down the back, feather-like secondary gills have been developed around the anal opening.

181. Some nudibranchs have developed fringe-like projections on their backs called **cerata** (approx. 1½in.). These carnivorous nudibranchs exhibit one of the Animal Kingdom's most bizarre feeding utilizations. When eating Cnidarians, such as hydroids or anemones, the nudibranchs digest the fleshy parts of the polyps, but store the prey's toxic stinging nematocysts in their cerata for use in their own defense.

182. Photographed at Gordon Rocks off the Plaza Islands, these dramatic blue-striped nudibranchs (approx. 1¼ in.) are preparing to mate.

183. Detail of a geometric design on the back of a gulf star, **Oreaster occidentalis**.

184. Starfish are abundant in Galapagean waters. One of the most profuse and beautiful is the gulf star, **Oreaster occidentalis** (approx. 1ft.). This lovely starfish has bright reddish-orange spines that are very distinctive. The back side is an intricate geometric design in red and white.

185. The sunstar, **Heliaster multiradiata** (approx. 1ft.), is a multi-armed starfish that often tucks its short arms under its body hiding them from view. In this position, the starfish looks like a large black dome, covered with bright red knobs. It appears more like a short-spined sea urchin than a starfish.

186. Bright red blood stars, **Astropecten** sp. (approx. 7in.), are found in sandy areas, where they often bury themselves during the day.

187. The chocolate chip star, **Nidorellia armata** (approx. 6in.), is another of the commonly observed starfish found in Galapagos. Often they literally cover rocky areas.

188. The fragile star, **Linckia columbiae** (approx. 4in.), is common on rocky underwater cliffs. It is rarely found in symmetrical five-arm condition. The unequal length of the arms is attributed to the ease with which they break off, giving rise to its common name. This starfish exhibits amazing powers of regeneration. From a detached arm, a new starfish can grow in about six months! Although its mottled color may vary, it is often brilliant red. In the photograph, the starfish is moving among black cup corals.

189. Spotted stars, **Pharia pyramidata** (approx. 7in.), are another commonly observed starfish, seen in shades of purple or yellow. In the photograph, it is feeding on pebble corals, **Cycloseris mexicana**.

190. These beautiful, multi-colored Christmas tree-shaped appendages are actually the feeding radioles of segmented worms. The worm's body is hidden from view by the calcareous tube in which it lives. Called Christmas tree worms, **Spirobranchus giganteus** (approx. 1½in.), they are found throughout the world, but are especially profuse in Galapagean waters.

191. The slipper lobster, **Scyllarides astori** (approx. 10in.), looks like a throwback to prehistoric times. Photographed at night at Tagus Cove on Isabela Island, this slipper lobster is crawling past several colonies of endemic cup coral, **Tubastraea tagusensis**, their polyps fully extended.

192. The magnificent scallop, **Lyropecten magnificus** (approx. 6in.), is one of the most dazzling animals found in Galapagos. Its mantel (or fleshy lips) is a stunning red, interspersed with blotches of shimmering violet and intense blue eye spots. The mantel's resplendent appearance is further enhanced by an edging fringe of golden-cream-colored tentacles. Magnificent scallops are found primarily on the west coast of Isabela Island and around Fernandina Island.

193. Detail of magnificent scallop mantel.

H85 1994